This Night I Sup in Your House

Timothy Robbins

Copyright© 2020 Timothy Robbins
ISBN: 978-93-90202-79-9

First Edition: 2020
Rs. 200/-

Cyberwit.net
HIG 45 Kaushambi Kunj, Kalindipuram
Allahabad - 211011 (U.P.) India
http://www.cyberwit.net
Tel: +(91) 9415091004 +(91) (532) 2552257
E-mail: info@cyberwit.net

No part of this book may be reproduced or transmitted in any form or by any means, electronic, mechanical, photocopying, or otherwise, without the express written consent of Timothy Robbins.

Printed at Repro India Limited.

For Mike, my natural habitat.

Acknowledgments

Tipton Poetry Journal: "Better," "Tannenbaum"

Main Street Rag: "Fault Lines," "Weddings," "Shortly After His 38th Birthday," "Forkerts"

Blue Moon: "Winter Sunday"

Slant: "There, There," "Breaking the Diaries"

Poetry Quarterly: "Monarch"

Pinyon: "Courtyard," "Choosing," "Dyar"

Two Thirds North: "You are Sitting at the Table"

Cactus Heart: "Bowing"

Bayou Magazine: "Interim," "Handling"

Hanging Loose: "T¿t," "Wyoming," "How You Came to Me," "Contours," "Where did I Put That Poem?"

Saranac Review: "To Know and to Be Known," "Stephanie, Screens, Poverty of Hands"

Wisconsin Review: "Timber"

American Chordata: "It"

Earthshine: "Doogle's Banjo," "Asceticism and Luxuriance"

Adelaide Literary Magazine: "Utah," "Raphael," "Roles," "Alfred and Moses," "A Flare," "Dérouté," "Dolores Park, Dating Between Boyfriends," "Essay"

Toasted Cheese: "Manmade Drifts"

Cholla Needles: "Instruments"

Foliate Oak: "In the Sink"

HCE: "Getting into Character"

Badlands: "El Grito de Dolores"

The Wayfarer: "Vessel"

Kestrel: "I Change the Card on my Desk"

Contents

Better

I lived there well, but I
could have lived better.
I was with you but I could
have been within you.
The heatwave when we
slept on the floor
could have been hotter.
We could have sweated
out sins we weren't even
aware of. Had the floor
been harder, we might have
felt more support.
The fans, standing blandly
by like eunuchs
could have breathed on us
fresher sweetness.
Yes, the sweat we cursed
we could have blessed
and used to anoint our
waists. The Chinese
food we had delivered when
I was too sick and
you too tired to cook,
could have delivered
us from evil. We ate facing
but we could have fed
each other as bride and
groom give marital
blood and body, heedless

of crumbs or stains that
might befall tux and gown.
We could have
nourished each other
like the blessed dead
in the parable of Heaven
and Hell's similarity.
Remember the tornado
warning? The sirens sang
their sadness, taking all
the town for witness. That
could have been our lament,
the dissemination
of our fertile fears.
We gathered our valuables,
descended to the laundry
room and sat on the exercise
equipment for two hours
without television.
We could have done this
routinely without threat
of tornado, each time
reevaluating what should
be saved. Remember Mr.
Liang, how viewless his
basement office was?
We could have welcomed
him to our third-floor
balcony with its panorama
of Amtrak windows blazing
at night like speeding
TV screens, the trains
and the Huron running side
by side in a perpetual

dead-heat, while fowl of all
sorts stirred the air with
their bets. We left well but
we could have left better,
could have tossed a handful
of dirt into the dumpster
where we buried what we
could not keep.

Contours

I've long cherished the notion that
David's sketch of Marie Antoinette

en route to death was traced with an
Etch-a-sketch.

Or like a high school art assignment
was made with one unbroken snaking

un-looked-at line. In both cases,
I wonder where the line starts and ends:

from the tip of her toes to the nape
exposed for the swift surgery awaiting her?

From the nadir of her cartoonish
frown to the nadir of her cartoonish frown —

a full tortured circle, the severing of
umbilical cord and head?

I'm writing now because —
either I was surprised by the resemblance

between this famous propaganda and
a drawing I made of you this morning —

or the resemblance was unconsciously
planned. In both cases,

I spent an hour debating where I
would begin and end my meditation.

You, fuzzy from a head cold, nose
dripping, wrapped in your heaviest blanket,

are not at your best. The queen's ugly
bonnet is an obvious and political

allusion to the rococo hats of her heyday.
Your knit cap is part of you —

your head more faithfully guarded
than the head of the most orthodox Jew.

Conversely, Marie's unrelenting posture
is part of her, part of her royalty,

the only remaining part — while your
stiff spine is ephemeral. Your

mother's been nagging you again. The
great difference is — wanting always to

look you in the face, I have drawn you,
not in profile, but as though I were the TV

you squint at. The great similarity is:
David's urge to humiliate and

mine to adore
are both power grabs.

Fault Lines

My fault the swollen uvula, the
rusty nails posing as relics, the
ethical impasse with Venetian
Carnaval masks, the obscene love
letters fed to mail slots; not locking
the door the night all the stars
pointed to burglary, choosing
to get laid rather than help a friend,
my parents' aging Christmas-less
knees, sunsets like busted
taillights, nights gooey as oil spills,
romantic frauds, the frog-eyed kid
who left unsatisfied, not giving
encouragement to a talentless
busker, the volcanic pimple on my
ass that scared off the handsome
spanker, losing my brand new
hushpuppies, spiking the Korean
guy's beer, not eating the pork chop
laboriously prepared for me, not
staying awake all night on the
corrugated roof, not striving for
organic unity, not insisting on organic
produce, having a Godzilla-sized
carbon footprint, leaving a pallid
molted rubber on the storeroom floor,
making my sixth-grade buddy think
our friendship was a psych experiment,
pushing sad men's hands from my thighs.

Handling (blood patch)

The emergency room doctor has the
nerve to ask *how* I became positive.
I'm in too much pain to be a smart ass,
to tell him I was just born optimistic.
He's going to syphon blood from the
crook of my arm and push it into a
wound in my dura mater. Blood
that could kill him will kill my pain.
The wound was a gift from a doctor
who laid me belly-down on a tower
of pillows, arching my back like an
outraged cat. It was so painful I soiled
the table. My blood pressure fell like
a house into a sinkhole. In the earth I
am a fetal curl. You are spooning
me. Then easing a cushion under my
pelvis (the French say basin). Then,
parting me with a breath on my neck,
your life enters me as easy
as a peaceful death.

Winter Sunday

Enough wind to stir the firs outside my
window, not enough to blow fine snow
from the roofs. I'm listening skeptically
to Beverly Sills trill, "Sweet mystery
of life, at last I've found you!" Sunday
is no Sabbath when faith and work run
out. Still, through some vague but
powerful habit of feeling, it's cozier
under this blanket than it will be
tomorrow morning. If I count right —
it's hard to hear time over Bubbles
Silverman belting one out — that was
seven chimes from the Arts and Crafts
clock in the living room. Whatever their
number, they stir an image of the hours
my dad spent building the clock, alone
in the garage, hot from a wood-burning
stove, listening to Terry Gross, so
autonomous he could be in the Black
Forest. Fifteen minutes later the first
Cambridge Quarter invokes quiet hours
working at his elbow. Sometimes on
broken Baldwins that put food on the
board, sometimes on mission style
tables — toil that was its own reward.
The half hour moves us back to the
January he photographed me feeding
ducks on ice, recalling and foretelling my
attraction to surfaces that crack, however

handsome, however nice. Third quarter:
It's the 1970s. He hangs a tangle of
Christmas lights, mod holly and ivy,
above his and Mom's pillows. Wired to
the radio, an electric miracle, they throb
and blink in sync with Donna Summer's
disco; they pulse with Barry White's
sultry nights.

There, There

"When you get to the trailer park, drive till you find a
candle on an ironing board on the front lawn. It won't

be bright. Little more than a star. Still it will be the
only one." Such were the directions you gave to the

post-concert party in the early eighties when Dylan
cast off his dark glasses as though they were a log, that

he might squint at the Light of the World, that he
might scold the rest of us for our specks. This snapshot

of you standing behind that board, so feebly lit you're
one with the night, is a companion to this video of Bull-

winkle's Charity Drag Pageant. Homely, but not dowdy,
in housecoat and curlers, with long strokes of an Ace

High Silver Star you keep time as you sing, "Such
are the dreams of the everyday housewife." Tomorrow

was always our dancing day. Sometimes in line with
the women's softball team. Sometimes just the pair of

us braving an empty floor. Once it was a stray soldier
who, like a WWF wrestler preparing to body-slam a

challenger, lifted you to the disco ball and slowly
revolved as you sang "God I think I'm falling." I

used to sing for you in your nomadic trailer. I was
sixteen. You were green from teacher's college. You

didn't mind my octave-jumping voice, pimple-pricked
face and assurance I would be the next Dylan. I was a

happy hobo in your aluminum boxcar with its books
in inspiring languages, African masks and poetry of

Negritude, rain sticks, real rain rattling in the down-
spouts, a ceiling that made you stoop like you were

hiding in an attic or had eaten the cake of self-loathing
that says, "Eat me." The trailer followed you like

shame to Muncie, Greensburg, West Lafayette, Bloom-
ington — and would have followed you to Morocco

if spirits could cross water. A Djinn waited in the S
trap and the evil eye peeped through the kitchen

window in the face of a welfare grandmother (who
ran your phone bill through the roof). The incubus of

homophobia hissed obscenities till you started the long
bike rides that hardened your calves like railroad ties.

The rest of you remained as soft as the marshmallow
peeps you ate from the sidewalk (maybe with some

incoherent notion you were not depleting the world's
store of nutrition). Soft as the sofa where I slept after

This Night I Sup in Your House

a one-month-stand's failed wrist-slitting, after
a hernia-stitching that robbed me of laughter, after

I drove the kindest harpsichordist I'll ever know
into the hands of, between the knees of the jealous

first-chair cellist. "There, there honey. There, there,"
you cooed.

Monarch

In his groin I find the last butterfly
tucked between the tapering of his abdomen
and the silk of his inner thigh,
the hollow that keeps ink warm
as though the dripping needle
has just withdrawn.
I can't shake the feeling
I am the monarch felled by migration
the next generation must end.

Courtyard

Where I come from only signs
linger on street corners and the
only girls who solicit are
scouts once a year at the IGA.
Rue Faubourg National, rubbing
against the train station, makes
me feel cosmopolitan. I need

a month to understand the
women on my street. I like to
see them looking as official as
the Police Municipale, tapping
the gendarme's tricouleur
épaulettes with tiny handbags,
running palms along nightsticks.

I like the way they defy autumn's
chill in their miniskirts and
décolletés, some flat-chested as
flappers, others, exemplars of
il y a du monde au balcon.
One middle-aged lady in a long
fur coat, taking care not to

sully her costly pumps, reminds
me of Bea Arthur. A blonde with
a wrinkled brown chest, like
she's had too much Côte d'Azur,
lives downstairs. She and a

colleague block the entrance
one night. The stranger

propositions; my neighbor
intercedes. "Il habite par ici."
"Je m'en fiche, tant qu'il paie."
I'm shaking so, the key, like a
schoolboy, misses the lock.
My neighbor takes it, gently
as one frees a loaded pistol from

a child. As the door squeaks open,
for an instant I see Versailles: all
the red velvet a brothel could
wish, mirrors as long as
Aphrodite's legs, golden lions
rolling balls lit by slender white
tapers. And there on the throne,

the Queen of Street Walkers, eyes
closed, head tilted, lost in Jean-
Baptiste Lully. Through the door-
way, into the pigeon-wet courtyard,
I mount to my garret and lower
"Hunky Dory" into the player I
bought from FNAC.

Choosing

1.

Today I chose — I think it was my choice —
to watch George Burns and Gracie Allen
on YouTube. George steps out of
what is obviously a set, assumes the mantel
of a cigar-tapping Greek Chorus, commenting
with self-deprecating affection on Gracie's simplicity,
masking the truth that when Gracie hears language
in surprising ways, she is a poetess.

2.

I looked up Ezra Pound's "The Tree" online.
David had emailed me that one of my poems struck him
as Poundian. Seems Pound and I both want to
become trees. The difference is Pound dreams of
restoring Greek gods and their metamorphoses,
of acquiring arcane lore and talking about it in archaic language.
I just think trees are sexy, and want to make love with them.

3.

An unconscious feeling that I'd
betrayed Nathan Birnbaum caused me to
download a collection of Yehuda Amichai poems.

4.

The show's first audience (which I
picture in black and white) couldn't
have foreseen the shining widower
George Burns was to become, staying

lit like his beloved Productos through
a 32-year solo run, squinting at us through
black glasses the size and shape of
coasters, from the cover of *Cigar Aficionado,*
applauding the wife whose picture he
kissed every day.

Not his choice to go solo.
Not his choice to be the straight man.
Not Gracie's choice to be the funny one.
Not Pound's choice to fall in love with Mussolini.
Not Amichai's choice to be
neither one of the six million nor one of
the survivors. Not God's choice to choose
Abraham.

I wouldn't mind being
the widower George became, the unrepentant
comic and smoker buried with three stogies
in his breast pocket, one for past, one for present,
one for future; one for Larry, one for Curly, one
for Moe — choose your trinity, if you can.

You are Sitting at the Table

preamble
I keep thinking about the groom's side
and the bride's and how at the reception,
amid bad dancing to corny music,
in boozy informality (antidote to
ceremony) this segregation gets flushed.
The couple drives off to recuperate.
The newly connected families droop at
the first of many messy tables, beginning
the long interweaving of chronicles.

amble
North from the Cumberland Gap,
from the Ohio to the Big Blue River,
Chrysler attracts and a girl remembers
a school where spellings, hardy as wildflowers,
solid as *big,* lovely as *blue,* entered her world.
She remembers her father's lap.
The watch twirling, cajoling memories
of unforeseeable, punishing slaps.
Fleeing her village, your grandmother
is a fulcrum; the long pole
stretches before and behind her,
Older Daughter in the pioneering basket —
Young Daughter, lagging, balancing.
Car-less, his wife in labor,
Dad sprints to the parsonage.

The parson fills the doorway,
impatient as a comic to relay a new joke.
With Deborah's wisdom a kitchen voice bellows,
"Arnold, get them kids to the hospital!"
Enfants terribles. Two Vietnamese children
run naked in the street.
I never see the girl. I never see the boy.
She's a photo in a thousand papers,
on a thousand websites,
flapping featherless wings, rushing toward us with the
black cloud, the clothed, the uniformed.
He's a figment I conjure
from childhood tales you tell me
of a street purged by the morning's
dose of monsoon and unwary passersby
harmlessly doused from a hose
wielded under cover of your family's outdoor shower.

Eight thousand miles away
My brother and I wiggle through
a sprinkler's cold falling arches.
Barefoot, we dodge clover bees.
At the bathroom tap we feel balloons grow
heavy like bloated bellies.
Not to cleanse your feet, but to make them
deportable, your father leads you to the mosque.
It will take more than this to induce the Party
to brush your dust from its feet.
Seven years old in a camp in Thailand
you hold it in for weeks on end,
terrified of falling into foreign toilets.
You're constipated to this day.
In the attic of your aunt's house in New Orleans

This Night I Sup in Your House

you and your sisters warm
your hands on sewing machines,
piecework far past midnight.
When staying up late is still
thrillingly forbidden, Dad comes
to the foot of the stairs and calls up softly,
"Grandma, are the boys in bed?"
"Shush, you'll wake them,"
as we squeeze in tighter, one
on each side of her in that wide
green chair, eyelids struggling
with TV's relentless, beckoning flicker.

post amble
A poet and a mathematician
set up house midway across the Bridge of Birds.
You bring your numbers. I bring my words.
We both bring scraps of tales
to burn in a barrel at our forebearers' feet.

Bowing

When I was 14 I memorized *Invictus.*
All I remember now is, "My head is
bloody but unbowed." I think of all
the bowing I've done since then.
Escaping eyes of bigger boys
who seemed offended by my existence.
Aping the obeisance of adults when
a man in a pleated dress intoned,
 "Let us pray." Baring my nape to
barbers' clippers. Drinking from
mountain brooks. Standing solemn
as a medalist when a Saudi woman,
careful not to touch me, hung a charm
around my neck. Lowering my face
into men's laps. Getting down on my
knees and searching the carpet for
a stray baggie. Praying, actually
praying I'd never do that again.

Interim

The Japanese family across the alley left
the blinds up when they moved. Now
in the dark before dawn when the train
horn comes from all directions,
I look through their window and see
not one, but two squatting doppelgängers.
"Good," I think. "The room's not lonely."
At first we're in perfect sync, like
Lucy disguised as Harpo finding Harpo
in her Hollywood hotel. Daily they grow
away from me. This morning they wave
first, rise and pace while my legs
go numb folded under the coffee table.
They share a different kind of sync.
When one calls the other *hypocrite lecteur,*
both know it's a term of endearment.
When one drinks, the other swallows.
When one's tired, the other snoozes.
They sit at their laptops and improvise
linked tanka I will never read.

Tét

Fifteen days till Tét. There'll be no firecrackers,
no Ong Tao astride his giant koi. Whatever has
replaced the Jade Emperor, we, not the Kitchen
God, must make our annual report. The New JE
will know SCOTUS says we can wed. Even if
George Wallace blocks the courthouse doorway,
we'll simply walk through him as we'd walk
through any other ghost. JE knows that brilliance,
hard work, conniving and laying low brought
you tenure, which will keep us warm and fed to
the end of our days (assuming Scott Walker
doesn't get his way). JE knows my grandmother
died and you cried on your grandmother's
memorial when our morning sweet potatoes'
burned skin reminded you of her blackened teeth.
He remembers the year, just four years ago, you
and University of Michigan Hospital saved my life.
He'll have a vivid image of your index nervously,
meticulously tapping air bubbles from my
penicillin bags. He'll want to know what we've
done and plan to do with our good luck. Our
balance sheet — tenderness and complacency,
emotional loyalty and sexual infidelity — might
baffle him. Maybe we'd be better off with the
old Kitchen God. What could he report but that
we eat well, that I never neglect the pillbox on
the counter, that the kitchen is redolent of oil and
spices as I peel and slice and you stand at the
stove, skillet in hand, making shrimp do backflips?

Wyoming

His last morning, dressing before
the mirror, he listened to the radio:
Aerosmith didn't want to miss
a thing and neither did he. His
mother listened to *Good Morning
America* turned up loud in the
living room so she could hear it
over the dishwasher. In our house
the radio was talking to itself while
my dad shaved. Same thing next
day when he froze mid-stroke,
unsure what *All Things Considered*
had said: tethered to something —
but to what? A telephone pole? A tree?
A fence? And why the word tethered?
It woke echoes of tether ball and
a playground's innocent screams.

I don't know what the killers heard.
I picture hunters, their ears to ground
that's silent as a lifeless chest. Not
the chatty ground they actually pressed.

He was fireworks. The Fourth of July,
every Christian the Pagans burned,
every Wiccan the Christians lit up.
The excruciating light inside,
explosions accentuating the killers'
features. They felt Roman candles in

their chests and exulted. After the last
spark darkened, there was only
the sound of their panting, crickets
and tree frogs and a wind, soothing
and gruesome as a lullaby.

I write about the sky, pop songs and
talk shows because that is all I can
bear. Later my dad saw the accused
in orange jumpsuits, their blank
faces like so many faces he grew up
with, so many looks he was accustomed
to trusting. Many fathers and mothers
saw photos of the boy when he was
still alive and all they could bear to picture
was their touch closing his eyes.

Weddings

then…
Western tuxedos were my brother's touch
along with his cowboy boots and a torch song
by George Strait. "Just be thankful men
can't wear hats in church," Mom pointed out.
Trying on my tux, I noticed the mirror bays
in Minear's Clothing were as I remembered —
though the multiplication of my image no
longer menaced. The Brannock device
still evoked torture, but now I knew better.
My brother wrestled Andrew, his soon-to-be
stepson, into his suit, jabbed in the shirttail, stabbed
in cufflinks and shirt studs, tightened the string
tie that reminded Andrew of Colonel Sanders,
pulled the laces of patent leather shoes that
reflected ceiling lights, moons on glossy black.
In the vestibule we joked about what I should play
for the recessional. *Send in the Clowns?*
Comedy Tonight? I pinned my dad with a carnation
as though he were my prom date. Grandma,
wheeled in from the home, blurted over the vows.
A heckler of her own sanity, she decried, "the fatal
marshmallows nurses poison us with." The next
day, hung over, on bed's edge, I studied a photo
the family had never seen: me in a wide-sleeved
kimono with black and white striped hakama
standing much taller than usual in split-toe socks
and geta — a souvenir "for the kind American
who has befriended our son in a strange land."

now…
Drummers go before us.
Women bearing lit candles
walk with their backs
straight as the candles' flames.
The marhwa, Agni's fire, is kindled.
Around it we walk together.
Seven unwed friends paint
our faces, feet and hands with
sandalwood, turmeric, rose water.
We bathe in river and lake.
Your mother lays a garland
around my neck.
Mine does the same for you.
The bed is adorned with flowers.
Tobacco is offered.
Our families come with fruit,
clothes and gold in red boxes.
Half we keep, half return,
protection from greed and sign
we demand only as much as we need.
Broomsticks are burned.
Bamboo is sounded.

Tannenbaum (for Marvin Rowe)

Arbor vitae outside a Denny's window.
Across the parking lot white pines fan
high in the air. In front of the Motor
Lodge three cedars loiter, embarrassed
Christmas trees stripped of their rank.
Tannenbaum in piped into the dining room.

The town seems confused with the students gone.

In the first scare after the test results
you talked of tightening your life.
No more beer, cigarettes, or raves.
No days when you just forget to eat,
euchre till four in the morning,
making love till six, snatching two
hours of sleep before feeling your way to class.

You wanted to decorate your crib for
Christmas. A tree bigger than childhood,
bulbs the color of billiard balls more
breakable than eggs, lights that
reminded you of a town where stop, go
and caution all twinkled white.

The florist thought I was crazy when I asked for
the tree of life.

This morning I'm breakfasting alone.
The sunshine bleeds like the words

of Jesus in a red letter edition. You're
in Gary by now. For the first time in
your life you don't feel safe in your
mother's home. The danger is in your
blood. No amount of prayer, no crib,
no cross will change you to the
rose e'er blooming.

Where Did I Put That Poem?

To have Julian Freud's huge eyes
and make each detail afraid to budge.
To be a collection of details.
To be humiliated for the sake of
art, for the sake of the painter's peace
of mind, for his late-blooming bank
account. To be the moment
some museum-goer, content with his
taboos, gapes at the docent who's
just said, "That's the artist's daughter's
pudendum" as blandly as she would
say, "That's Titus van Rijn."

To Know and to Be Known

I need to know Allyson knitted
Heathrow's nightlife, serenely bored,
while reruns of "Hey Allyson!"
with its disarming non-sequiturs
played in her head. I need to be known
as the one who slept fitfully on the
floor which a janitor buffed, skirting
my body with his great fluffy buffer.
Stan needs to know Hiroki Kondo
rode the North Ridge quake to the
end of his sleep. His Asian muscularity
was that seismic-blasé. Stan needs to
be known as the one who still pictures
Hiroki shirtless in boxers, with long
valiant hair, groping for the phone,
groaning at his mom calling from
Osaka. Marta needs to know her older
sister is taping her office door so she'll
know if a colleague's penlight has tinker-
belled the dark boards. This, though
Marta betrayed their ancestral
paranoia. Walker wants to be famous
for his fearless year on half crackhouse
half regentrified Alabama Street —
and to be remembered by the john
bellowing in the alley, doused with
cold water from his fourth-floor window.
He needs the right man to see how he eased
a needle into the crook of his arm.

Stephanie, Screens, Poverty of Hands

They are poorer than Mother
Teresa, they who hear
one Yahweh. They ride Hiltons'
glass cylinders,
uppers and downers,
day after day, same hollow shaft,
same guests zooming in and out.
Muzak sugars their inattention.
Feigning class, they are like
the rich only in their wish for
everyone else to be poor.
Still their tiny bones yearn
for beats, intervals, tones
baffling to Yale's ethnomusicologists.
I myself filled this lift till
Stephanie cut the cables.
Heedless of gravity, it broke the roof,
a climax of glass and rubble.
I saw hung-over afternoons,
marshmallows charred like
platoons, *Gun Smoke* while
Houses of the Holy's falsetto
shook gnats from the backdoor screen.
Too young to lift the sound, I knew
I would pick it up when I was bigger.
She fell home late at night, drunk
and rancid with love, fell
naked on the only mattress left
for her, drunk and naked as Noah.

My brother and I tiptoed to the
kitchen as though for
water but really, like Noah's sons,
to sneak a violating peak
at authority's sleep. Hands opened
the fridge for its light.
Hands lifted the sheet. Now hands
that pull bark from the
eucalyptus will pull my skin from me.
Only when I see insensate strips
lying at my feet
will I know what it is. A fifteen-year
old wanted to dint the mattress.
A fourteen year-old wanted to be her
legs. In one theater hands smelled
of popcorn. In another they smelled
of K-Y jelly. In both, faceless
children abraded their skin on rocks.
How poor we are, climbing
from one past to one future.
The best we can hope for is to
make the path meander.
I think about the hands that
circumcised me. I suppose they
were gentle, not the hands of men
who shucked me like an ear
of corn. I think of the first hands
that cleaned me down there
and the last that will dirty me.
Hers were hands that took,
an art I never mastered.
I dream she's on trial. A scene
from *The Devil and Daniel*

Webster, silky black as a waistcoat,
white as lamplight on the dead
traitors' faces. One by one,
guilty witnesses testify.
A grandmother speaks of
unrepentant loans. A grandmother
complains of purse-prying lies.
Her mother recalls the dog-fighter
she left standing like a mannequin
at the altar. My mother speaks of
the time she dressed me in curls
and perfumed me with nicotine.
I wake up. She sits ross-legged
on my couch.

Breaking the Diaries

Her second husband hangs
with gulls and a Christ that lingers
after his cross decays.

She annulled him before
he could close that embrace
and we, the grandkids, knew
we were never to mention
his name.

She locked the license in
the trousseau she burned
with a tangle of storm-felled branches.

I wouldn't break her aluminum
Christmas tree or the seal
on her canning jars
or the promise I gave her
(it was tough as Swiss steak).

So why do I have no qualms
breaking these diaries?

I tell myself such simple keys
couldn't safeguard dark secrets.

And diaries embossed with
beribboned kittens

couldn't harbor more than
a farmer's wife's undying
lookout for rain.

Around the dining room table we
peer at the ghostly graphite. Not
an inch of paper un-inscribed
(Great Depression habits)
with old fashioned cursive wobbling
more after each apoplexy, dwindling
as her body shrank.

I am a writer and yet I'm perplexed.
Why the loyalty to these annals?
Even in the last years when we stopped
replenishing them December 31st,
she took to filling 3x5 notebooks.

With the aid of a magnifying glass,
Dad reads word by word
as though epoxying shards
of a broken pot.

About my parents
(always called "the kids").
About the Methodist Sunday
school that loved to tease their
token Baptist. About children
she once baby-sat now sending
their own children to daycare.
About a phone call from freshman
me with the remark that my
boyfriend and I "sure were mixed up."

Dad lays down the loupe and
closes the book, saying without words,
"some words shouldn't be magnified."

I don't tell him to keep reading.
The real events aren't recorded here.

How she blotted out the name
of the Antichrist. How she
fed more people than Jesus —
hundreds of the mentally ill at
Muscatatuck, hundreds of 5th and
6th graders at Jerman Elementary.

How she led Mrs. Evans
back to her husband
every time she wandered
into our living room.

How You Came to Me

Geese claim the skies as skateboarding teens
claim the sidewalks; as drunken ex-privates
carol in the dark till their voices crack;
as tourists from the latest prosperity
shout in duty-free shops, cocky in their unintelligibility.
I choose this river-bend because here even geese
are circumspect. They come for shallows
and soft level ground on which to lay their eggs.
The shapes of their legs, their long supple
necks, (curving downward to graze,
twisting to pick mites from their backs)
preserve their evolutionary past.
From a hopeful distance, I watch
a committee of five — worried, officious or
curious? — approach. Two veer to my left,
two to my right. The middle one keeps on,
sizing me up at each lurch, coming close enough
to catch bread I toss in his path. Briefly,
unreasonably he trusts, then waddles back,
honking delight, disapproval, bellyache.

Timber

His skin like quarter-sawn oak,
perfectly cut growth rings running

straight and tight the length of all
that is long or flat. I gaze on dark

swirls of medullary rays and discover
inner forms. Wavy interlocking grains,

evocative of entwined limbs,
meticulously buffed and brushed with

coat after coat of thinnest shellac. My
face shines in his dark glass. He holds

the finish, resists twisting and warping,
is impervious to degradation.

It

The Last time you heard Ann Sothern sing
"The Last Time I saw Paris," flowers
glinting on her earlobes and her veil,
made of and for the silver screen, saddened
you. The closest you'll come to the City of
Lights is the single postcard from a college
kid wafting like summer wind through
your factory thirty years ago. It was the
morning you woke and thought *Everyone
longs to be the gypsy bride or the rogue who
carries her off.* It was sitting on the patio,
snapping beans. A jet moved silently
across the sky and you absolutely could not
say why that silence woke your dormant
widowhood. The clever boy at your feet, so
clever you couldn't help worrying, suggested
it was because, in spite of the quiet, you
knew the jet was roaring. It was reading
Huck Finn and laughing helplessly. Reading
Aristotle and laughing, but that was probably
mostly the weed. There in the stacks more
ruled by hush than sanctuaries, laughing,
not haughtily but as a governess laughs at
her willful charge. It was standing with your
wife of fifty years, looking into the canyon,
thinking *time is doing the same to us only
we are more easily sculpted.* It was the last
time you saw Back Creek. The sons of the
same old men chawed outside the general

store and your son-in-law tried, in vain
you knew, to capture them on his video-cam.
It was the first night we slept here. Our
things hadn't arrived yet. The bare floors
held a thrill of welcome we were bound
to efface. It was your garrulous but not
usually eloquent parent announcing *it's a
privilege to be your mother.* It was the
first voice you heard as you recovered
from anesthesia: the mourning dove's query,
the embarrassed cough, campground
dulcimers, an irrepressible bottom smack,
air struggling to escape crêpe paper
threaded through spokes.

Shortly After his 38th Birthday

Ash up evening, mulling
over Ginsberg's heartache
over Dylan. Open the
leather-hinged box I keep
in musky shade, sure my
straight lover is sleeping
and won't heed.

On the day bus we're in
a palanquin. We see into
lowly cars and judge the
texters, enemies of
pedestrians, the woman
waxing her lips in the rear-
view mirror, the man
diapering his son at the stop.

At night, height and
fluorescence betray us.
We're busts of fallen tyrants.
We're frozen dinners and
the last, bruised,
picked over produce.

Doogle's Banjo

Maybe he had a real banjo at home,
leaning in a corner next to his spittoon
or hanging on a wall near a crucified
wooden spoon. Maybe when he played
air banjo for the junior high boys it was
more than imagined joy. Maybe he could
see the emptiness between his flailing
hands as an instrument, hear the noise
he made in his nose as ringing steel,
feel the strings press his calluses, feel
the taut drum's vibration against the butt
of his palm. Maybe the derision
I heard in the boys' voices was all in
my often bruised imagination. Maybe
their calls were music too. And if it
was meanness, maybe the Bluegrass in
Doogle's head drowned it out.

Asceticism/Luxuriance

In autumn our river trees turn to
asceticism, fasting down to the last twig,

shedding leaves as though they were
passions, weaving carpets of decay.

They do this without hesitation in
order that the river, which serves them

all year, might have its season to shine.
And shine it does, for five proud months,

slate tinted through the day, attended by
a humble sun, black at night with bracelets

flashing on its arms, snow like ermine
draping its shoulders till spring returns

and the trees' humility is rewarded, the
Buddha born a prince once more.

Utah

1.
I like to think you'll find me limp
on the floor, light enough to be
picked up with tongs. If you have
trouble locating my bangs, look
with the same anger that kept you
on hands and knees whenever you
thought someone had swiped your
mislaid baggie. Spread me in every
state: solid, liquid, gas, even Utah.
Shotgun my essence to the mourners
(feign kiss or rescue if necessary).
The woman who swallowed wine
only once and that in ignorance, who
eased her calves and shins before bed
with witch hazel and my sins. The
woman who joyed in my foolishness
even more than I did. ("Someone's
getting stoned in the stairwell." I
called 911 to report a lapidation.)
The man who is as close as man
can come to disembodied memory,
whose recollections are all the eternity
I can endure. The kid who terrified
me in the dark of our shared bedroom,
whose arm protectively scything
my shoulders when the guide doused
the light in Mammoth Cave redeemed
darkness. The archetypal homeowner

who promised one last traipse over
his cerebrum's salt flats, whose scared
fist sank into my face rewarding us
both with the shock of familial satori.
The Great Contrarian who greets me
every morning with "More and More
two-headed sharks are popping up,"
news of ever-expanding camaraderie

2.
I withheld the names to slow you down.

Raphael

Raphael, pushing CVS glasses on
his face, has forgotten the price
of Renaissance specs. He's working
on a *Holy Family* — as soft, as
dreamed as an early masterpiece.

I'm on a cushion. Mom's on the
ottoman. Between us, backgammon
spears aim at each other.
Dad reads and toe-strokes my
shoulder. The composition is

stabler than a dream, not as stable
as a painting. On the shelf, Grandpa's
firm throat is framed by his navy
collar. His cap is a dark halo.
His mouth is sensual and humiliating

like a uniform. His left hand rests on
the left leg of my father's baby overalls.
The buttons on Grandma's blouse
like cows in a field attract the child.
Sharing a mind, Mother and son

fix a point off to the right. Readers
are strewn throughout the flat —
some with the crossed arms of

Egyptian slaves in 1960s Panavision.
Some with arms extended in

welcoming rigor mortis. Did I
get these poses from bath-houses?
Hypocrite lecteur, when you read
readers did you think I meant you?
These holy trios, would they be truer

in the desert's unflattering light
or in the cramped dim where the
Frankes held their breath? Something
or someone, not Herod's or Hitler's
horsemen, comes for us. No dream

in Dad's head urged us to flee
to these stanzas. We remind me of
Ling from China, Miguel from Peru,
their adopted boy from the Ukraine:
excited, unclear messages.

Roles

More convincing than Alec
Guinness, Peter Sellers, Max Baer,
I play multiple roles in this film.
There's one part I can't point out
myself. That's the one I've become.
For decades I railed against Joyce's
obscurantism. Now I start my
mornings with an audiobook of *Ulysses,*
and the passages I enjoy most are
in languages I don't speak.
I find myself longing for Greek,
whose alphabet I can't recite.
Like starting over. Being four again,
looking forward to following
my brother to kindergarten.
Another three years till piano
lessons. Mary Legenhaus, who
smelled of tobacco and hairspray
and the huge bag of dog food
she kept in her Chevrolet.
I mentioned her, separately, to my
parents. "One hell of a lady. One
fantastic woman. Taught two
generations to play." Words in
lockstep, like Republicans on the
Sunday news shows. And then,
to back it up, the story of her
handling a drunk in a nightclub
with blistering elegance. She

taught me to play "Just Like a
Woman" (she taught me to play
just like a woman) before the
name Dylan meant anything to me.
Said it was his most melodic song.
"Nobody feels any pain." Someday,
when there's no one left to say it,
that line will be true.

Alfred and Moses

(for A.E. Housman)

I picture a Merchant Ivory flick.
Young classicist with patrician cheeks,
face of an Arabian prancer, features
precise as a Latin declension.
His friend, the rowing Blue, with a
Clydesdale jaw and nostrils that boast
they can sniff out spoony beastliness
behind any doll-sized lapel.
The athlete's swagger is drawn to the
scholar's snub as though they were
opposite sexes. Something in his Great
War poems tells me: mother, father,
sibling, bride, the gay poet, lingering
at sick bedside — all have a flower only
they can lay. Something tells me the gray
flesh, peeping from under the sheet,
reminds him of Moses at the end of
a race, in a teammate's lap, abs heaving,
tears flowing, handsome face clenched
and unknowing. He's thinking of shells
undressing soldiers and occasional
poems, re-dressing them for wakes.
He's remembering when he exploded
his love in their lodgings and in Moses'
eyes his famous paeans to bravery
were twisted into shrapnel pornography.
Already Moses strides British Columbia

haughty as rowers bearing sweeps to
the Thames, silently shouldering
Union-Jacked crates.

A Flare

She invited ex-bride's maids
to her Wedding Dress
Burning. The silk/rayon
blend smoldered like grassfire,
shone like a witch at the stake,
blanched like the moon at
a woman's wedding with
her Self. I wondered if their
faces reddened, if their eyes
shot red sparks. I remembered
a guy I picked up. How
he flickered behind a tube
with a pebble called the
Devil's Eye stuck in one end.
His complexion enraged
others who don but don't burn
white veils and gowns, though
they do burn other
darker symbols.

Dérouté

The route to her home of
fifteen years is suddenly
as faint as the Appian Way.
She doesn't notice
the change. Past Fire Station
One (there is no Two),
past the Church of
God (no Church of the Devil)
where Pastor Robert Browning
preaches without an
Elizabeth, past the dress
factory (a long brick barrack
that hasn't sewn a stitch in
twenty years),
past grape arbors
kids raid after nightfall
(the Concords slip from
their skins at the gentlest
pinch), up our front
steps through the unlocked
front door. My grandmother
finds her mentally
cataloging the furnishings
like a drunk slowly
waking in a strange room.
Why is the floor so soft?
Why are the ceilings too
low and getting lower?

Half an hour later Grandma
sees her on her hands and knees,
crawling up the steps,
a penitent atoning for a
sin she can't remember.

Dolores Park, Dating Between Boyfriends

A bronze priest squints. His furrowed brow casts
a protective shadow over his eyes.

Lito. His nurse-y voice, Hallmark promises in
Tagalog and belly swelling with compassion.

A bronze bell hangs between two white arms
in line with palms and the busy street. I was afraid

to touch it, lest the kindness spill out and be wasted.
Lime-colored parrots loop tree to tree, swoop

past the Mission where Jimmy Steward stalked in
Vertigo. Oh, what's the point of lying after all

these years? I didn't want his belly pressed to mine.
Everywhere you look, look again. Our beautiful park,

wasn't named for the Mission two blocks north, tourist
monument to Spanish domination.

William. Also Filipino. Handsome as J.D. playing
Huck Finn to my Tom Sawyer before his parents

shipped him to Culver Military Academy. El Grito
de Dolores, The Cry of Sorrows rends the air.

Freedom fails to mend it. Something about me
William didn't want to press against. The priest,

hand on his outraged heart, is Padre Hidalgo,
Father of Mexico.

A Chinese chemist in Palo Alto. Caltrain actually
passed under a rainbow, a high-speed, tuneless

game of limbo on the way to a weekend of sacrificial
lobsters and yellow Calvin Klein briefs falling

from a bed that remained aloof from the floor.
This high ridge we call Castro Beach,

whose view reaches past downtown and touches
the bays, was once a Jewish cemetery. The dead

were moved not for being Jews but because
the precious real estate of this city belongs to the living.

A Buddhist named *Steve,* drinking tea in my rocking
chair, wants me to strap him to Samsara's Wheel.

Essay

I can only approximate his Malay
name. Can't picture the sturdy
Mohammedan face he rested on
classmates' shoulders. The heat
must have felt immature, amateurish.
Indiana was a new country for him,
as teaching was for me. He wrote
simply, longingly of a hairdresser's
half-repressed smile, of her nails on
his scalp making the locks' black
stingray undulate in the watery sink.
His lids met like fingertips
extinguishing a flame.

Manmade Drifts

I whisper to myself. It's
more effective than
talking. Stripping away
the vowels, reducing
verbal music to a fit of
breaths is often the only
hopeful choice. At 3:00
a.m. a snow clearer warns
me: Not all voiceless
utterances are soft. In an
Oscar winner I saw last
Wednesday, a boy, with
violence surprising
from such skinny arms,
blocked his mother's
hate-fueled screams
with a sliding glass door.
Boy and viewers —
though we weren't lip-
readers — easily read
faggot! I wake and
see my husband's mouth
doing, as usual, the work
of his nose. I doze and
rouse to his breath on my
eyes. It's been so long,
the kiss surprises like
an expletive, scrapes

like a plough, exposes
where we are, clears the
way for where we'll go.

Instruments

Snakes. They go to technical schools
to learn their amazing skills. Some
train themselves through grueling
snake yoga to remain unfurled and
stiff. They are used as walking sticks,
which explains Moses' famous trick.
In that case they were instruments of
escape. Some learn to imitate
harp strings. The harp makers' skill
is to choose serpents of the right length
and to keep them from growing or
shrinking. This morning I feel
ashamed of the instruments in my
room. Even if I could plug them in,
they would sit there dumb. Even if
they were touched by fingers and
thumb, the music (not their own)
would not equal the fan's quiet,
cooling drone. Occasionally I find
the humility to be the instrument of
my mother's gardening, parting a
Richmond rose's labia to sic light
on the beetle within, its back like our
pills only slick and Japanese.
Identical opposites are unwieldy
but beautiful instruments. They are
unusual in that they can be tuned by
thought and only by thought. The key
is finding the right thought. For

This Night I Sup in Your House

instance: Harpo found hiding
behind his instrument, the strings
drawing perfectly straight silver-
white scars at precise intervals
on solemn cheeks that moments
later will expand like two alarmed
spike-less blowfish. I tried —
if I'm honest not very hard —
to make the guitars, the mountain
dulcimer, the soprano and baritone
ukes in my walk-in closed (converted
to music room) instruments of my
hands. I see from their disappointed,
conniving glances they are plotting
to make my hands their violins.

In the Sink

Granny on the draining
board, breakable as china.
(Keep Palmolive away from
Dad. He thinks it's a Greek
wedding.) Granny in the
sink vacant as Depression's
bare Christmas floors and
promises she canned and
stored in the pantry. Feet
in the drains, she trembles
like cut flowers while someone
goes to fetch a vase. Something
not too showy. One hand on
the tap, the other on the transom,
she looks for the source of a voice
calling, "Nannie Prewitt, come
down from there. This night I
sup in your house," while
another scolds from behind,
"Mom, you don't have to
clean the windows."

Getting Into Character

Often, before Luke speaks, there's
a long silence — thirty minutes
to an hour. Once in a while, it's days.

Other people don't realize words
are forming. They don't see the
link between his not-speaking
and his narration. I see it because
his face becomes a stage with the
curtain lowered between scenes.

I hear the stage crew's shoes
scuffle like guests at a surprise
party prior to dousing the lights.

I hear the sound of armchairs on
castors and cityscapes gliding down
like squeaky angels.

The curtain rises and actors
launch into lines they've acted a
hundred times while the
audience (usually me) hopes for
an inspired impromptu or a
mistake to revive its interest.

The lead-up to doubts and
recriminations is different and
briefer — a matter of seconds.

His face wears its
backing-out-of-the-driveway
frown. He shifts gears
without looking down, and
inches toward me where I wait
inexplicably in his righthand lane,
my left.

Usually, he brakes. I get in and
buckle up. I think how handsome
we'd look in sashes like maharajas
at a country club. I think of tied-back
curtains in a parlor where a séance
is about to start.

He aims the remark at the wind-
shield as though to defrost it. I turn
and answer his cheek.

We ignore the other me in the
backseat remembering the few
times the bumper nudged
my shins, wondering if some day,
against all odds, he will
stomp on the pedal like it's
the first cockroach.

Forkerts

Backyard Dyer splits firewood —
man putting asunder — the soul's
halves falling away from one
another, each to a landing that
suits it — to peace. The logs'
outrage reverberates from every
house and garage, the neighbor-
hood easy in its role as echo
chamber. On her knees, weeding,
Mom notices the rail splitter's
frown and, jocular, comments,
"They're making you work for
your living," unclear herself who
she means by *they*. Dyer pulls off
one glove as though to throw it
down, wipes his brow backhanded
and says, "Married a packrat."
Meaning Judy, who has filled his
home, who keeps tabs on: the
Browning boy who lost half his
arm joyriding too close to a guy
wire, who gets along but dreams
the severed limb co-stars in *The
Addams Family*; the Hubbard girl
who succumbed to a seizure alone
in the rented symbol of her self-
reliance, who lay on the linoleum
waiting in vain for the wooden
spoon she'd been stirring with
to climb between her teeth and

stop the invisible priest using
her tongue for her last rites;
The Fitzgerald who took the cloth,
his brother who drove the church
from the temple, their sister who
ran for mayor, their sister who
survived an alcoholic car; the Fox
who went off to war and brought
the battle home to the auto
factory. Judy goes door to door
till the last summer when she has
to receive visitors in the hospital.
The first thing out of her mouth
is always *Tell me something new.*
Tell me everything that's new
with you. The second funeral is
harder than the first. It takes days,
weeks, months. No unctuous
professional helps. Every empty
can in the larder, crippled,
redundant tools in the garage,
packaging, magazines, gutted
envelopes — all are uninvited.
The whole attic is hauled to
the landfill. There are rooms you
can't walk into, rooms you have
to strip away layer by layer.
At the first funeral you wear
elegant black and people stand
ready to wipe your tears. At the
second, you wear your filthiest
rags and there's nothing to wipe
but sweat and no one but yourself
to wipe it.

Dyar

His kids were my companions in
the first illusion of eternity. Their
yard was ours and ours was theirs
and we were all guardians of the
northeast corner of the block we
thrived on, a promontory lording
it over a residential sea. One
summer afternoon he donned
a latex mask and came running
gorilla-like, scooping us one by
one from Mother May I, catching
us in the middle of a scissor step,
sinister-laughing us into the kitchen
to shampoo our sweet smelling
hair in the sink. The mixing of
our giggles with his diabolical
guffaw, sagging latex features as
sad as they were scary, arrival of
a rapture so unexpected it could
never be repeated — all these
tricked us into believing the
raids went on intermittently,
Viking incursions all summer long.
Despite this, despite camping
trips replete with fire-making
tutorials and sticks whittled
by blade and tale, and campers
folded and unfolded easy as
Swiss army knives, Mr. Forkert

remained one of my childhood's
steadiest embodiments of the
Other, one who approaches
but mustn't be approached,
equal of strange churches'
ministers. It had to do with
his resemblance to ladders,
which I always feared — with his
going off to The Bank every
morning while other fathers
went to shops, factories,
garages — his clockwork drink on
the way home from work and
my image of him hunched over
the bar first like a streetlight whose
bulb flickered and buzzed —
later as a goose-necked desk lamp
with a short in the switch.
Whatever it was, it's gone now.
I visit in the summer, see him
struggling with the lawn mower,
his dark form moving from
window to window, the only
movement in the house. It's
gone but it's too late. When I
cross the grass to give the
ritual greeting, there's no way
around the sadness, the
solemnity of an audience with
a monster brought in from pasture.

El Grito de Dolores

Every spoken "spo" or "ken,"
if you're reading aloud —
every stray noise — light
on paper, light through the screen
— sticks and humps of every
letter up to this point

was the poem.

The rest is the pseudonym
my family gave me,
signed without flourishes.
A knife-thrower's knives
outlining his partner's bravery.
White tufts blowing through
tough-love bootcamps.
"Argentina 1970."
No right to say *that* with
one high-heel half-off,
the other heel, a bounty
hunter's ripped up license
escorting white moths over
megachurch parking lots.
My sweat is on your
cheeks, reminding them
of my thighs. Medically
speaking, it's dysphagia.
I've swallowed enough
and won't swallow more.
For ten years I sat in the park

with Ted Dagnese. Sun-
bathers mistook us for a
hyperrealism masterpiece
of privileged queers.
The last day taught me
his dad left his mom for
"a nice guy," and she
never remarried. The priest
with his hand (a large
white moth) over his heart
(a dark moth in a cage)
is Padre Hidalgo. My
parents and teachers
told me poetry was
precious and useful. I say,
if you want to get use
from this, copy it longhand
and take it to a hand-
writing analyst.

Vessel

Too long since I threw the fridge door
open wide and heard from inside the
crisper the muffled sound of onions
singing a shanty about a plucky vessel.
Since I cracked the freezer door letting
out a faint ballad: *The Doom of the*
Endeavor and the Rescue of her Men.
Since you and I talked about the first
wine and its first vessel — the unlike-
lihood of their being, the miracle of
their meeting, the sweetly comical
trial and error as each guessed at its role.
Too many days without the pleasure of
pronouncing *vessel* — the lower lip
teasing the 8 and 9 incisors, the
sibilant blowing the soft vowel into
the liquid L. I can't even recall the last
time you answered the door and I
hollered, "Who is it?" And you
bellowed over your shoulder, up the
stairs, "I don't know, but she appears to
be a vessel of good will," which was a
relief — or "He is clearly a vessel of
peril," which was exciting. Will we
ever again pray in a becalmed vessel
or kiss in a vessel redolent of apples?
Isn't it time we took out the vessels in
the closets, divested them of their

newspaper, washed, dried and polished
them with every vessel-loving inch
of our flesh?

I Change the Card on my Desk

Who are you? That, I know. You're my chosen
one for the day. Who you were, I can't say.
Your back is bossy (correspondence here:
stamp here: name and address here:) but
uninformative. This could mean you were
forgotten or lost or were bought to be treasured
or were so sinister a drugstore owner was
saving you for an enemy — but who sends
postcards to their foes? Judging from your
sepia and the style of your clothes, I suppose
you are dead by now. With your suit,
your straight stance, your arms at your
sides, you could be on display in the parlor,
you could be a lionized figure lying in state.
Maybe I think this because you're lying on
my desk, stiff as your detachable collar.
Here, let me prop you against the mug
with the definition of friend on its circular
wall and its crowd of pens struggling to get
out. Now you could be standing in the line
leading to that leader, the citizens so close
together they could be chained at the ankle.
I promise to fight my urge to unclasp your belt
while you hold still as a photo or at least as still
as a hero posing for a daguerrotype, if you will
convince me with a hallucinated nod that the
cause of your squint is the desire to see if
I'm someone you know. Who sends postcards
to their foes? Is this the secret everyone

knows and for once in our lives we manage
to keep? Must have been a thousand
"Desolation Rows" (heard and sung till it
could sing itself in my sleep) before I learned
"They're selling postcards of the hanging"
isn't Dylan being surreal. Since then I've
tried not to fill in the details. Did a Klansman
tote the Brownie? Did the youngest run
back and fetch it or did they return the
next day — no need to hurry — it wasn't
a crime scene — no need for a flash in
sunlight. What thoughts went through
minds at the printing presses or postmen's
minds, house to house? Till today, I assumed
those paper trophies were sent to kith and kin.
Just as I assumed this stranger so like my
grandfather and great uncles was mine to
collect although it wants to be sent, to assume
my name and bear my message to one who,
like me, lucked out.

www.ingramcontent.com/pod-product-compliance
Lightning Source LLC
Chambersburg PA
CBHW051806130726

47987CB00003B/1133